Celebrating Diversity & Equity in the Classroom

Zak Books, 2010
Oakville, Ontario

Published by Zak Books
Oakville, ON Canada

www.cutestfacebook.com
www.zakbooks.com

 2010 Zak Books
Noncommercial-Share Alike 2.5 Canada
You are free to share, copy, distribute and remix this work.

Printed and bound in Singapore
13 12 11 10   4 3 2 1
First Edition

Library and Archives Canada Cataloguing in Publication

Zak, Rebecca, 1983-
The cutest face : celebrating diversity & equity in the classroom / Rebecca Zak.
32 p. ; 20.3 cm

ISBN 978-0-9813991-0-2

1. Cultural pluralism--Juvenile literature. 3. Toleration--Juvenile literature.
2. Difference (Psychology)--Juvenile literature. 4. Picture books for children.
I. Title.

HM1271.Z35 2010   j305.8   C2010-901872-9

Book design by Dave Zak.
Illustrations were hand painted in oils.

To: Dave ♡

There's the morning bell.
It's picture day today!

Here come my students, all looking their best.
I can't decide who's the cutest!

First through the door is Vrajesh.

He has a big smile on his face, as usual!

Vrajesh never stops smiling all day long.

Chantae has also just arrived.

She has some new beads in her hair today. Those will look pretty for her picture!

Next is Maria.

She lost a tooth last Tuesday.

That will be a good memory to look back on in her photo!

Callum came to our school from a place called the United Kingdom.

I'm so happy to have him as part of our class.

I bet Zoë could tell me who the cutest furriest face belongs to!

Her guide dog has a sweet and gentle temperament.

Jordan says he doesn't know how to smile, but I know that's not true!

We'll get him grinning in time for his photo.

Amrinder is also new to our class.

He's making friends right away because the kids can tell he's nice.

Kiyah has brought in a drawing she made of how she thinks her photo will turn out.

I see she has drawn in her braids! Very good job.

Reem has artwork to show too, but it's on her hands.

Her mother has used special dye called henna to make beautiful designs.

With so many unique students, how could a teacher like me pick one cute face over another?

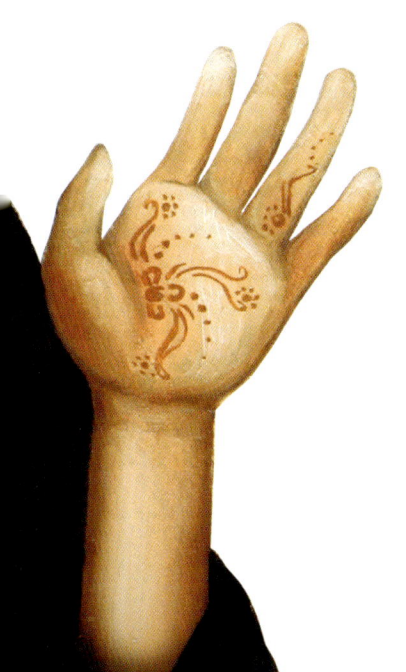

Jean-Pierre has the ability to speak two languages.

I wonder how he would say "cheese" in French?

David doesn't know if he wants to wear his glasses in his photo.

I tell him he should because that's what makes him look like David!

Jessica and Brittany
are best friends who
are always together.

Sometimes I call them Jess-any because they're so inseparable!

Juan says his dad made him brush his teeth twice so that his smile will be extra bright. Looks good to me!

Cooper likes to laugh a lot.
He just giggles and giggles.

The photographer won't have any trouble getting him to smile today!

Siyanda and Siyabonga look so much alike, I don't think I will be able to tell their photos apart!

They are identical twins...

and identically cute!

Angel is the smallest of all my students.

She may be little, but she has a very big heart!

Now it's the time we've all been waiting for...

SAY, "CHEESE!"

All my students are so cute in their own way...

but what's best is how cute
everyone looks all together.